History

A review of inspection findings 1993/94

A report from the Office of Her Majesty's Chief Inspector of Schools

London: HMSO

Office for Standards in Education
Alexandra House
29–33 Kingsway
London WC2B 6SE

Telephone 0171-421 6800

Contents

Introduction

This subject profile for history provides a review of the findings from inspection conducted for and by OFSTED during the academic year 1993/4. It continues the publication by OFSTED of subject reports focused on the quality of provision made for and standards in history. It extends information and discussion to include aspects of inspecting history which are of direct interest to inspectors and may be found relevant by schools.

The evaluation of standards, quality of education and provision for history is based on evidence from the inspection of 56 primary and 360 secondary schools. The secondary schools were inspected for OFSTED by teams led by Registered Inspectors and the primary schools by teams led by Her Majesty's Inspectors of Schools (HMI) and usually containing independent inspectors in training.

In addition, evidence from the inspection of history in primary and secondary schools by history specialist HMI was used to assist in the interpretation of patterns emerging from analysis of the main body of inspection data.

Subject Report

Main Findings

- In relation to the capabilities of the pupils standards are satisfactory or better in around seven out of ten lessons at Key Stage 2, eight out of ten lessons at Key Stages 1 and 3, and nine out of ten lessons at Key Stage 4. For Year 12 and Year 13 the proportion is nine out of ten lessons. Standards are good or very good in almost two lessons out of ten in Key Stage 2, three out of ten in Key Stages 1 and 3, almost four out of ten in Key Stage 4 and almost half of the Year 12 and Year 13 lessons [paragraphs 1 to 10].

- Within this broad picture there are significant variations: In Key Stage 2 standards are higher in middle than in primary schools; in secondary schools standards in relation to pupils' capabilities vary markedly between different ability groups, particularly in Key Stage 3 [paragraphs 1 and 6].

- The pupils generally attain a higher standard in oral than in written work. Other than in Key Stage 4, the pupils do relatively little extended writing [paragraphs 4 and 8].

- Although the quality of teaching is satisfactory or better in eight out of ten lessons in Key Stage 1 and seven out of ten in Key Stage 2, there are significant variations within most of the schools [paragraphs 15 to 20].

- In some of the secondary schools National Curriculum history is being implemented in such a way as to narrow the range of their teaching to the detriment of quality [paragraph 18].

- The assessment of National Curriculum history remains problematic. In particular in some of the schools statements of attainment are treated over-mechanistically. In making their judgements teachers place insufficient emphasis on the need for the pupils to demonstrate their achievement at particular levels by drawing commensurately on their knowledge from the programmes of study [paragraphs 21 to 27].

- The assessment of Attainment Target 2 is largely unsuccessful [paragraph 21].

- Although history makes a positive contribution to the curriculum in primary schools, the Key Stage 1 Programme of Study is sometimes not fully taught and in Key Stage 2 the curriculum is often planned in such a way that the proper links between the programmes of study and the attainment targets are insufficiently developed [paragraphs 28 and 33].

- The quality of curriculum planning in the secondary schools remains very uneven [paragraph 36].

- Insufficient attention is given to the pupils with special educational needs [paragraph 37].

- In Key Stages 1 and 2 there are usually co-ordinators for history, but the role of the co-ordinator is often less effective than it might be because of lack of time, the combined weight of responsibilities and a passive approach to the role [paragraph 38].

- In all Key Stages there are particular imbalances in the types of resources used. In Key Stage 2 poor use is sometimes made of project loan collections. In Key Stage 3 there is an undue reliance in some of the schools on textbooks, which has a narrowing effect on the subject and depresses achievement [paragraphs 43 to 45].

Key issues for schools

- In Key Stage 1 schools should build on their success in implementing National Curriculum history by ensuring that the full programme of study is taught.

- In Key Stage 2 more detailed planning is needed to ensure proper treatment of the study units, with clear links between the material in the programmes of study and the attainment targets.

- In Key Stage 2, in particular, closer attention should be paid to ensuring that the tasks which pupils are set support their learning in history effectively.

- There remains a need, for secondary schools especially, to set the requirements of the National Curriculum within the context of their own aims, objectives and departmental strengths.

- In all Key Stages schools should seek to develop their understanding of assessment in history.

- In all Key Stages there is a need for schools to balance their resources for history in order to provide maximum support for teaching and learning.

Standards of achievement

The GCSE and GCE results achieved nationally in history in 1994 are tabulated in the Annex to this report.

Key Stages 1 and 2

1   In relation to the capabilities of the pupils standards in Key Stage 1 were satisfactory or better in eight out of ten lessons; and in Key Stage 2 in seven out of ten lessons; standards were good or very good in around three and two out of ten lessons in Key Stages 1 and 2 respectively. In Key Stage 2 standards were significantly higher in middle schools than in primary schools.

2   In Key Stage 1 work of a high standard had particular features related to the Programme of Study and Attainment Targets. The pupils used the vocabulary of historical time in the context of the study of their family or their environment; they were beginning to make inferences from visual sources and artefacts; and they were able to tell stories accurately. Where standards were poor it was often because tasks were restricted to low-level activities such as colouring, or because the pupils were not given the historical context which would have enabled them to advance their knowledge and understanding. As a result, the pupils showed little grasp of the idea of time, were unable to retell stories accurately and could not establish a sequence.

3   In Key Stage 2 the best work was achieved where the pupils had developed a strong knowledge base, had established an understanding of change and causation and were able to compare differences between

societies (Attainment Target 1). In addition, they had begun to analyse and evaluate a range of types of historical evidence (Attainment Target 3).

4   In general, the pupils reached a higher level of attainment orally than in their written work. In particular there was insufficient extended writing to support the development of increasingly complex knowledge and understanding. Standards were depressed where the pupils either had insufficient knowledge of the period to inform their work; or, conversely, where the focus was exclusively on the acquisition of factual detail.

5   Generally the pupils showed an interest in history and were keen to learn. In Key Stage 1 good learning was characterised by the quality of the pupils' contribution to discussion, and the way in which they posed questions. In Key Stage 2 where learning was good the pupils increasingly took the initiative in investigation, applying themselves critically to a range of historical sources. Learning was poor where the pupils used historical information mechanically, and especially where they merely copied sources of information.

Key Stages 3 and 4

6   In relation to the capabilities of the pupils, standards of achievement were satisfactory or better in eight out of ten lessons in Key Stage 3 and in nine out of ten lessons in Key Stage 4. In Key Stage 3 three out of ten lessons were good or very good, with almost four out of ten in Key Stage 4. Standards at these Key Stages varied markedly between different ability groups. They were satisfactory or better in almost nine out of ten lessons where the pupils were in the upper ability range, and good or very good in more than four out of ten. In middle and lower ability groups, however, the figure was seven and two respectively. Where the pupils were taught in mixed ability groups standards were satisfactory or better in relation to capabilities in eight out of ten lessons, and good or very good in three out of ten.

7   A key feature of work where standards were high was that the pupils acquired and displayed knowledge and understanding, relating it to their previous learning. For example:

- in Attainment Target 1 the pupils were able to explain and account for change over time, identify and interrelate causes, and make comparisons between the periods and societies that they had studied. Achievement was most secure where the pupils wrote fully and provided relevant detail.

- in Attainment Target 3 the pupils increasingly applied their skills in the evaluation of evidence in order to make judgements about the reliability and value of sources, to make inferences and to produce judgements.

8   In a significant number of lessons, even where standards were in other ways satisfactory, poor achievement was characterised by responses which lacked specific factual detail, were directly copied from the textbook or other reference books, or which did not go beyond the literal comprehension of sources. In a number of cases where the pupils achieved high standards orally, this was not replicated in written work. Extended writing, and particularly writing in response to investigation or open questioning, was infrequent – particularly at Key Stage 3.

9   Standards in Key Stage 4 were high where the pupils were able to deploy their detailed knowledge accurately and appropriately, both orally and in writing. The pupils were able to establish cause and consequence, ordering and linking causal factors and justifying their judgements. Evidence-based work demonstrated a sophisticated understanding of the nature and problems of historical sources. Much coursework was very good, including the detailed use of visits to historical sites as the basis for investigation.

10   Work in the minority of lessons where standards were poor lacked purpose. The pupils' range of knowledge was narrow and their responses were superficial.

11   The quality of learning was at its best in upper and mixed ability classes. In Key Stage 3 high-quality learning was characterised by a positive approach to history. The pupils were fully engaged in work of different types, responding in whole class sessions or contributing actively in groups. They considered historical questions carefully, applying their knowledge and skills to new situations. They also raised their own questions, developing and testing hypotheses, and

undertaking investigations, both of particular sources and of open ended questions. Study skills were increasingly applied as the pupils moved towards public examinations. Notes were well organised and supported learning, and extended writing was well planned and structured.

12   Learning was poor and progress limited where the pupils were not actively engaged with the historical information on which they were working. They failed to make the most of the opportunities afforded to them and were content to restrict their responses to culling information or to minimal responses. They did not ask questions in order to develop their understanding of concepts.

Post-16

13   Post-16, standards in relation to pupils' capabilities were satisfactory or better in over nine out of ten lessons and good or very good in half of Year 13 lessons and four out of ten Year 12 lessons. In part this may be explained by the fact that, in a significant number of lessons, Year 12 students were having difficulty in adjusting to the new demands of A-level. Where standards were high, the students were able to draw on detailed knowledge and understanding of history and historical methodology and to apply it in their analysis of sources and questions. The students were able to play a part in informed discussion and to develop and support hypotheses.

14   In general, the students applied themselves enthusiastically to historical questions, engaging in informed, detailed and sustained discussion. Study skills were applied in the making of notes and in structured essay writing. The students read with purpose, engaging with an increasingly challenging range of texts. In the small minority of lessons where the quality of learning was poor, the students were passive and their main activities were restricted to listening and uncritical note-making. Reading was limited and study skills were poorly applied.

Quality of teaching

Key Stages 1 and 2

15   Overall the quality of teaching was satisfactory or better in eight out of ten lessons in Key Stage 1 and in seven out of ten in Key Stage 2. Within most of the schools, however, the quality was variable. In Key Stage 1 good teaching was characterised by clear planning within the framework of the study unit, careful choice of accessible resources, and a proper balance between narrative, explanation and questioning. In Key Stage 2 the best teaching showed a firm command of the subject material and the use of historical detail to inform and enthuse the pupils.

16   Generally poor lessons, and lessons which in other ways were satisfactory, were characterised by one or more of lack of clear purpose, over-emphasis on direction by the teacher with no opportunities for pupils to consolidate their knowledge, lack of differentiation and inappropriate resources and tasks. In too many lessons provision was insufficiently challenging, and did not build effectively on the existing capabilities of the pupils.

Key Stages 3 and 4

17   In Key Stage 3 eight out of ten lessons were satisfactory and over four out of ten were good or very good. Overall the teaching of higher ability classes and mixed ability classes was better than the teaching of middle and lower ability classes. At best, the teaching had clear purpose, employed a range of strategies, and maintained a good balance between lively and knowledgeable exposition and challenging tasks matched to National Curriculum objectives at appropriate levels. A range of resources was used. High expectations were shared by the teacher and the pupils. Overall, the best teaching provided a rich diet of history which satisfied the requirements of the National Curriculum in the context of the particular strengths of the department. In particular, success came where the teachers continuously and critically evaluated their work in the National Curriculum, ensuring that changes arising from implementation made good sense and enhanced the quality of work.

18   Where teaching was less satisfactory the purpose of lessons was unclear, and in particular the attainment targets of the National Curriculum were neglected. There was a general lack of attention to differentiation. At worst this saw classes doing the same work which was unchallenging to some of the pupils and inaccessible to others. There was on occasion a lack of input by the teacher, with an over-reliance on textbooks and school-produced resources, often resulting in a monotonous diet of low-level questioning and over-directed learning. More specifically, there was a neglect of historical evidence, with neither an appropriate range of material nor a sufficiently broad view of the way in which skills in evidence should be developed. In some cases where poor teaching was attributed by the school to the effects of the National Curriculum, the teachers had adopted new methods uncritically, or had narrowed the range of their teaching to the detriment of quality.

19   In Key Stage 4 teaching was satisfactory in over eight out of ten lessons and good or very good in over four out of ten. Good teaching had clear objectives and a clear sense of purpose, satisfying the broad aims of the subject as well as explicitly meeting examination requirements. Explanation was skilful and knowledgeable. Tasks were carefully set to develop understanding and exercise skills. Resources were well chosen, contributing towards a challenging diet. Due emphasis was given to strengthening the pupils' examination technique. In a few poorer lessons the pupils were not motivated by the teaching, which was narrow and repetitive, with the weight on the acquisition rather than use of information and with insufficient depth of study or exercise of skills.

Post-16

20   Teaching was satisfactory in nearly nine out of ten lessons and good or very good in nearly six out of ten. Usually teaching was expert and highly knowledgeable. There was a good balance between imparting information and challenging the students through their learning. Notes were well structured, and based upon good study practice. Variations of teaching style – exposition, questioning, guidance – were effectively employed. There was a proper focus on the needs of the examination, and especially on analytical writing, the use of historical

evidence and historiography. In a minority of lessons the students were not sufficiently challenged, and in some cases there was insufficient recognition of learning needs, especially at the start of sixth form courses.

Assessment, recording and reporting

21   Assessment of National Curriculum history continued to be generally problematic. There was increasing confidence with Attainment Target 1 and Attainment Target 3, although even here much assessment was tentative. The key problem, especially in Attainment Target 1, was in establishing the extent to which knowledge from the programmes of study must be used in support of statements of attainment in order to demonstrate achievement at a particular level. The assessment of Attainment Target 2, however, was still the major difficulty, and little successful practice was seen.

22   Assessment remained under-developed in Key Stages 1 and 2. Where the 1992 non-statutory task material was used, it was seen to have a beneficial influence. In general, however, much assessment remained informal and *ad hoc*. Insufficient attention was often given to setting tasks which promoted understanding and skills in a way which could be properly assessed. There were many instances of poor quality marking which failed to address historical matters. As a consequence records were often unhelpful, and reporting to parents rather bland.

23   In Key Stage 3 much marking was clear and constructive. But there were two particular concerns: the literal use of statements of attainment; and attempts to target discrete statements of attainment. Both approaches failed to provide effective learning objectives and were a cause of confusion. Some departments relied solely on formal testing in order to provide information on the pupils' attainment. Such tests often gave only limited information and failed to acknowledge the full range of the pupils' achievement.

24   Although, in general, assessment of National Curriculum history has been problematic, some strategies were employed which appeared to be more successful. In particular some departments nominated specific tasks for assessment. The pupils' responses were used to inform

the teachers' understanding of levelness and for standardisation purposes. This increased the teachers' confidence in their judgements. Other departments found it useful to set work with attainment targets as broad objectives, but to trawl through the pupils' work in order to gain an overall view of individual pupils' capability.

25 The quality of record-keeping was highly variable. In a number of departments which had adopted quite complex recording systems, difficulty with the practice of assessment caused them to be abandoned, with a reversion to pre-National Curriculum methods. The quality of reporting to parents was generally satisfactory.

26 In Key Stage 4 the teachers were able to build on existing experience of the GCSE. Some very good coursework assignments were seen during inspection.

27 Assessment at A-level was generally good. Comment on assessed work was usually of a high quality, with a focus on the analytical skills which underpin work in history at this level. Commonly, however, the students' day-to-day notes went unmarked and unchecked.

Curriculum content

28 Planning for National Curriculum history remained a matter of difficulty for many of the primary schools. The quality of curriculum documentation was often poor. In Key Stage 1 history was generally found within broad topics and, whereas this could work well, the relative contribution of history to a topic became insubstantial where it was not carefully planned, with the result that the full programme of study was not taught.

29 In Key Stage 2 history was part of a range of curriculum structures: as a separate subject; within history-focused topics; and within broadly based topics. Given careful planning it was possible within each of these structures for schools to meet National Curriculum history requirements. Many of the schools had established a whole school planning strategy for history, but in a number the choice of study units was made by year groups or individual teachers. Such an arrangement rarely worked well, and contributed towards an incoherent course of history, particularly where it was not taught as a separate subject.

30   Many of the teachers found that history-led topics proved highly successful vehicles for other work. This was sometimes demonstrated by the considerable amount of time used, directly or indirectly, for history. The amount of time given to history varied considerably, and was complicated by the fact that much of what happened in designated history topics was in practice only indirectly related to the study of history.

31   Supplementary units sometimes received less time than they should have been given. On occasion, study units concerned with aspects of the past over a long period of time were fragmented, with elements taught at intervals across the whole Key Stage. Where whole school planning was effective this appeared to be a successful device, acting as a spine for the whole course. Where planning was ineffective the content of such study units became decontextualised and meaningless to the pupils.

32   Where there were middle school structures, there was usually a clear apportionment of study units between the first, middle and upper schools. This arrangement was generally adhered to.

33   Lesson planning often failed to link the programmes of study to the attainment targets. Rarely was due attention given to the differing learning needs of the pupils within the class. Where the schools operated a two-year rotation of topics, there were rarely sufficient devices in place to ensure coherence and progression.

34   In the secondary schools the great majority of history teaching took place as a separate subject. Where there were other arrangements, such as humanities courses, history was usually a discrete element within the course. On occasion the blocking arrangements which this required led to an unnecessary amount of non-specialist teaching.

35   The amount of time allowed for history in the secondary schools ranged considerably. The requirements of National Curriculum history were entirely or predominantly met in almost all of the schools. In some of the schools insufficient time was found to deliver effectively the supplementary study units. This was sometimes because of the lack of time overall, and sometimes because core units had received a disproportionate emphasis.

36   Curriculum documentation was highly variable in quality. At best there were clear statements of aims and objectives, including the National Curriculum, and detailed schemes of work which properly displayed the relationship between the Programmes of Study and Attainment Targets. In many cases, however, documentation was meagre, often consisting only of statements of content or planning grids which did not provide sufficient detail. In particular poor documentation gave insufficient support for new and non-specialist teachers and failed to provide an overview of progression in history through the school. There was also insufficient attention to matching tasks to the capabilities of the pupils.

Provision for pupils with special educational needs

37   Often insufficient attention was given to the particular needs of children of different abilities, and especially of those who found reading and writing difficult. The quality of resources and the pitch of tasks were commonly inappropriate for those pupils with special educational needs; although in some of the schools and departments parallel sets of good-quality resources had been developed to meet the needs of such pupils. Some of the support teachers were well used, providing access to mainstream activity. In other cases, however, their purpose was unclear and they were not well deployed.

Management and administration

38   In Key Stages 1 and 2 most of the schools had a designated co-ordinator for history. But the advance in the role of co-ordinators noted last year does not appear to have been sustained. Many co-ordinators had received sufficient INSET, but in a number of cases had not had the opportunity to disseminate it to the other teachers. Often responsibility for history was in combination with other subjects or aspects, and little or no time was available to fulfil the duties effectively. More often than not the co-ordinator acted only as a point of reference, writing the policy document and providing resources and advice on request.

39   In most, but not all, of the secondary schools there was a designated head of department. The quality of leadership was highly variable. Some departments ran well despite the informal nature of their working. Many of the most successful departments combined clear working arrangements with good teamwork. Formal structures included a handbook with departmental policies, clear and agreed schemes of work and a schedule of meetings. Good departments had established clear priorities. In a minority of departments, however, structures such as these were not in place. Documentation was poor, arrangements were *ad hoc* and there was no clear development plan. In most departments, including many otherwise successful ones, there were no arrangements for monitoring the quality of work in the department.

Resources and their management

Teaching staff

40   Most history in Key Stages 1 and 2 was taught by class teachers, many of whom had no qualifications in history. Often, however, unqualified teachers were very effective and shared their pupils' enjoyment in the subject.

41   In the secondary schools the majority of lessons were taught by history specialists, although in most some history was taught by non-specialists. Often non-specialists were well supported, but it was sometimes the case that they were disadvantaged in terms of resources and accommodation as well as expertise. In some of the schools the timetabling arrangements were a cause of poor match, for example to support blocked timetabling for humanities programmes in Key Stage 3.

42   The provision of in-service training in history, as experienced by the teachers, was very varied. Some had found many opportunities for attendance at courses in order to gain information or professional development. But in some of the schools the only in-service training had been internal. This isolation had, in some cases, compounded misunderstandings of aspects of National Curriculum history and its assessment arrangements.

Resources for learning

43   In Key Stages 1 and 2 resources for history were rarely adequate. Although some of the schools purchased books to support implementation of the National Curriculum, often these were only single copies to provide the teachers with ideas. There was, in some of the schools, a heavy dependence on school-produced resources, often of poor quality. Activities which limited the pupils to comprehension and close questioning sometimes appeared in this form. Project collections, often library loans to support a particular topic, were a key resource. Although such collections are associated with investigative learning and personal research into aspects of topics, in practice they were often chosen inappropriately in terms of the books available, and were not used with sufficient care.

44   Good use was often made of artefacts, of the particular experiences of local people and visits. Audio-visual aids were often well used.

45   In Key Stages 3 and 4 resources were inadequate in a large number of the schools. Few of the schools had appropriate textbooks in sufficient range and number to support the effective implementation of National Curriculum history. In some of the schools textbooks were used uncritically in a way which had a narrowing effect on the quality of work in the department. In many of the schools there continued to be heavy reliance on school-produced resources including photocopied material and worksheets. Although some of these were of good quality, many were poorly presented and did not support effective learning. The opportunity to use such resources for matching tasks to the capabilities of pupils was often not taken up. In a significant number of the schools, too, the range of resources used was narrow. Some of the schools relied heavily on video recordings, whereas others made little use of this medium. Information technology remained under-used in many of the schools, often for lack of access to hardware. At best, the teachers employed a range of appropriate resources including text, audio-visual material, artefacts and visits to historical sites.

Accommodation

46   In Key Stages 1 and 2 the pupils were almost always taught in their own base rooms which were often extremely good learning environments, with display consisting of the pupils' work, posters, photographs, and artefacts. In some of the schools history was so successful that class displays permeated the corridors and public areas.

47   In the secondary schools the majority of teaching took place in specialist rooms, some of which were well used and supported the quality of work in the subject. In other cases, however, history was taught in rooms which were inadequate in size or organisation – including technology workshops and science laboratories.

48   A tangible constraint for many of the teachers was the limited access they had to information technology rooms and to the hardware which they contain.

Inspection issues

Inspection development

49   Inspections carried out under Section 9 of the Education (Schools) Act 1992 began in September 1993. Inspection teams have made a good start in meeting the requirements of the Framework for the Inspection of Schools; they have become more confident as the year has progressed and early uncertainties have been resolved in many cases. This part of the subject profile draws together some of the key issues for further improving the quality and standard of inspection. Many issues are similar from one subject to another; where there are subject-specific matters these are indicated.

50   Some examples of inspection writing are included. They are not intended to be viewed as models or templates but illustrate how Framework and inspection documentation requirements can be reasonably met.

Evidence gathering

51   Inspectors generally sample a good range of history work of different year groups, abilities and key stages across the compulsory years of education. They usually achieve a good balance although the time allocated to inspecting history varies considerably. It is important that where a school has a sixth form, post-16 work is fairly represented in the sampling.

52   In reaching their judgements, inspectors use evidence from a good range of sources. It is important that clear reference is made to them in support of judgements in records of evidence. The Supplementary Evidence Form provides a means of documenting evidence and judgements from sources other than lessons and could be more widely used.

Lesson Observation Forms

53   Overall, Lesson Observation Forms are completed conscientiously, with attention to the relevant evaluation criteria. Inspectors could usefully check that subject detail and characteristics are incorporated wherever possible.

54 In relation to the **content** of lessons, the majority of inspectors adequately indicate the topic of lessons usually with reference to the National Curriculum Order. Further details of the lesson activities would be helpful in setting the context. An example of a 'Content' section from a Lesson Observation Forms follows.

Year 5, mixed ability

Different activities were taking place: AT3 Using sources to compare forms of sailing ship over time; AT1 Making comparisons of similarity and difference speculating on cause and consequence based on comparison of Roman and Viking ships.

55 Inspectors draw on their professional knowledge and experience to make overall judgements about the **achievements** of pupils. Responding to the Framework requirements to assess pupils' achievements in relation to national norms and taking account of pupils' abilities has not proved easy. Revised requirements and guidance published in June 1994 should help inspectors in making these distinct judgements. To support judgements it is important that inspectors clearly identify and record what pupils know, understand and can do and set achievements in the context of National Curriculum Statements of Attainment. Some examples of 'Achievement' sections from Lesson Observation Forms follow.

Year 8, mixed ability

Achievement (age referenced): A lesson on The Gunpowder Plot: Standards average in use of sources in AT3. Some inferential thinking. Work touching on AT2 demonstrated understanding of how popular account/historical record might come to differ. Satisfactory knowledge of events and context of Gunpowder Plot, and understanding of related concepts. Grade: 3

Achievement (taking account of pupils' capabilities): Standards of oral responses consistent with mixed ability nature of class. Pupils' written work below that previously achieved (as indicated in exercise books). Some work incomplete, much that is scruffy. Lack of factual detail; inaccuracies; keywords misspelled; sources not fully explored. Written work consistently weaker than standard of oral answers. Grade: 4

56   Clear evidence of pupils' attitudes to learning and their behaviour in lessons is usually given, and this is reflected in the grade given for **quality of learning**. Greater prominence should be given to other attributes of learning, particularly pupils' progress in lessons and those aspects of learning in history included in section 6.6 in Part 4 of the *Handbook for the Inspection of Schools.*

Year 5, mixed ability (working on transport through time)

Very high motivation. Good collaboration over tasks. Pupils showed ability to use an index and dictionary accurately to locate information; care in selection and interpretation of information. Pupils persevered with challenging tasks; testing increasingly perceptive hypotheses against the available evidence which was added to during the course of the lesson.

57   Inspectors usually cite relevant evidence when judging the **quality of teaching**, and evaluation is based on the criteria in the Framework. They need to check that the full range of criteria is used, including teachers' command of the subject. In the following examples, a number of attributes of teaching are referred to.

Year 7, mixed ability (working on the Roman Empire)

Clearly stated aim. Good teacher knowledge. Teacher led whole class discussion with good use of open questioning to review work of previous lesson. Supported pupils as necessary whilst they considered range of documentary and pictorial sources individually or in pairs; followed by whole-class discussion of outcomes. Good use of questions to explore opinions. Overall a purposeful, well ordered lesson. Differentiation by outcome. Clear direction and high teacher expectation in evidence.

58   The Lesson Observation Form could be more widely used to indicate contributions made by the subject lesson to key skills and to learning in other areas of the curriculum. It also provides opportunity to signal the impact of contributory factors on achievements and the quality of learning which can be drawn on when compiling the Subject Evidence Form.

Subject Evidence Forms

59   Subject Evidence Forms are usually fully completed, very often thoroughly and thoughtfully. In most cases, a wide range of evidence appears to have been used. Inspectors need to check that reference to this range of evidence is sufficiently explicit in the relevant sections of the Form and to ensure that the emphasis is towards evaluation rather than description.

60   Particular attention is given to aspects of standards of achievement and the quality of learning and teaching although, as in Lesson Observation Forms, in considering the quality of learning more emphasis is placed on pupils' attitudes and behaviour than on their skills as learners. When commenting on examination results as part of their evaluation of standards of achievement, inspectors should ensure that the evidence includes the basis for any comparisons with national data.

61   Completed sections from Subject Evidence Forms follow. They deal with standards of achievement in a secondary school and quality of teaching in a primary school. They provide adequate evidence for producing the subject section of the report.

Standards of Achievement

Standards of achievement at GCSE are good and well above the average for schools of this type. In 1992 over 85% of pupils obtained a pass at grade A–C compared with 47.4% nationally for comprehensive schools. In 1993 over 78% obtained one of the top three grades, with 4 out of 19 obtaining grade A. Standards of achievement were satisfactory or better in all lessons observed, in relation both to pupils' capabilities and national norms. Pupils' factual recall was good. They showed a good understanding of cause and effect and the processes of historical change. The majority of pupils were able to examine and assess the relative importance of different historical interpretations. There were good examples of both oral and written work. Many pupils were able to make provisional evaluations and interpretations of complex historical information. Pupils generally were very confident in their approach to work in history.

Quality of Teaching

History was taught largely in the context of broadly based topics. This approach was not always successful in ensuring proper coverage of the National Curriculum. Much of the work was resource-based, but some of the tasks were poorly chosen. They did not allow pupils to develop the range of historical skills. In general there was a focus on the programmes of study with insufficient attention to the attainment targets. In some classes there was a heavy reliance on commercial materials, and insufficient thought had been given to ways in which they could best be used.

62   When considering features such as the resources for learning, management and the quality of teaching, the emphasis should be on evaluation of the effects these have on the standards achieved and the quality of learning. The following extract from a 'Contributory factors' section of a Subject Evidence Form deals with assessment in a secondary school. It includes clear judgements about features of provision and some indications of their effects.

- *Assessment results are recorded in portfolios which contain samples of pupils' work.*
- *Portfolio data and items updated termly.*
- *Portfolios not widely used (as yet...a new system) for planning, targeting or for monitoring progression and expectations across the key stage.*
- *A number of tasks are clearly labelled by AT and SOA but not consistently.*
- *AT1 and AT3 targeted by teachers, but not AT2.*
- *Some attempts within year groups to standardise assessment.*
- *Evidence of attainments is not fully secure; judgements based on evidence that lacks depth, particularly in Key Stage 3.*
- *Marking, annotation and explanatory comment generally poor/inconsistent and pupils do not have a clear enough idea of how well they are doing.*
- *Comments on reports to parents tend to focus on attitudes and approaches rather than on historical understanding and skills.*

Judgement Recording Statements

63 The Judgement Recording Statements are usually fully completed. Inspectors need to ensure that all available evidence is considered in arriving at judgements for inclusion in the proforma. The purpose and use of Judgement Recording Statements are outlined in Appendix C of Part 3 of the *Handbook for the Inspection of Schools*.

Subject sections in inspection reports

64 Most history subject sections in inspection reports meet the Framework requirements and those seen well matched the evidence in the Subject Evidence Forms. They give appropriate emphasis to standards of achievement and the quality of learning and teaching. Inspectors need to ensure that overall judgements are clear and succinct and draw on all the evidence available, and that factors which impact on standards of achievement and quality of learning are clearly identified.

65 The following extracts from reports illustrate writing about standards of achievement and the quality of learning.

School A

...Standards in history range from good in some aspects of the work to less than satisfactory in others. In both Key Stages 1 and 2 standards as a whole are satisfactory in relation to national expectations but not in relation to the capabilities of the pupils. In Key Stage 1 pupils are developing a language of time and are able to retell stories from the past and answer questions about them. In Key Stage 2 pupils in most classes demonstrate good knowledge of the period they are studying and can refer to other study units to establish a chronology. Older pupils are also able to discuss causes and explain the importance of particular events. These standards are not reflected in the quality of written work, which is often fragmentary, sometimes copied, and fails to address appropriate historical questions. In particular, pupils' understanding and use of evidence is less than satisfactory...

School B

...In Key Stage 3 standards of achievement in history are a little above average in terms of national norms. In relation to the pupils' capabilities standards are satisfactory. Pupils generally show a secure knowledge of important events and personalities within the period studied and a firm understanding of key historical concepts. Pupils undertake a good deal of extended writing, much of which is of good quality and is carefully presented...

School C

...The quality of learning is invariably good. Pupils make identifiable progress in terms of knowledge, understanding and skills; they maintain high levels of concentration and perseverance; they generally are enthusiastic and enjoy their work. Pupils take the opportunities offered to show initiative, manage and take responsibility for their own work. This reinforces confidence and develops learning skills. Good use is made by pupils of opportunities provided for them to discuss issues together...

Subject performance data

66   Tables of the GCSE and GCE results achieved nationally in 1994 are appended.

GCSE results for 15 year olds[1] for History 1994

Type of School		Number of 15 year old pupils entered	1994 Percentages achieving grades									1994 Average points score[3]	1994 % A*-C grades	1994 % A*-G grades	1993 Average points score[3]	1993 % A-C grades	1992[2] Average points score[3]	1992[2] % A-C grades
			A*	A	B	C	D	E	F	G	U							
Comprehensive		168893	2.0	8.8	17.0	20.4	16.1	13.7	10.5	6.3	3.1	4.37	48.2	94.9	4.11	47.6	4.17	47.5
Selective		9250	7.0	26.5	33.9	21.0	7.5	2.5	0.8	0.4	0.1	5.92	88.5	99.7	5.81	88.5	5.77	86.4
Modern		5255	0.2	2.6	8.9	17.5	18.8	20.0	15.2	9.9	4.3	3.62	29.2	93.1	3.36	29.1	3.45	29.0
Maintained	All pupils	183398	2.2	9.5	17.6	20.4	15.7	13.3	10.2	6.1	3.0	4.43	49.7	95.1	4.17	49.1	4.21	48.3
	Boys	86752	1.6	7.7	16.2	19.9	15.9	14.0	11.3	7.3	3.9	4.25	45.3	93.9	3.95	44.4	3.99	43.8
	Girls	96646	2.7	11.1	19.0	20.8	15.5	12.7	9.1	5.1	2.1	4.59	53.6	96.1	4.37	53.3	4.40	52.4
All Subjects Maintained	All pupils		2.1	8.4	16.4	20.5	18.9	14.5	10.2	4.5	1.5	4.40	47.4	95.5	4.12	46.3	4.14	45.0

1 Aged 15 on 31/8/93
2 1992 results include a small amount of data from special schools
3 Calculated on basis A*=8, A=7, B=6, C=5, D=4, E=3, F=2, G=1

– less than 100 candidates
* more than 100 and less than 500 candidates
x information not available

GCE AS results for History 1994

Type of School		Number of candidates	Percentages achieving grades							% A–B grades	% A–E grades	Average points score[p]	1993 % A–B grades	1993 % A–E grades	1992 % A–B grades	1992 % A–E grades
			A	B	C	D	E	N	U							
Maintained	All pupils	386	6.0	10.4	12.4	16.1	19.2	13.2	20.7	16.3	64.0	1.6	12.2	55.1	16.6	60.1
	Boys	141	7.8	7.8	14.2	17.0	17.7	17.0	15.6	15.6	64.5	1.6	14.9	57.7	18.4	60.4
	Girls	245	4.9	11.8	11.4	15.5	20.0	11.0	23.7	16.7	63.7	1.6	10.6	53.5	15.2	59.8
All subjects Maintained	All pupils		7.1	10.2	14.8	17.9	18.2	12.9	15.1	17.3	68.2	1.8	17.0	65.5	16.6	65.4

– less than 100 candidates

* more than 100 and less than 500 candidates

p Calculated on basis A=5, B=4, C=3, D=2, E=1

The number of pupils taking AS levels is insufficient to yield a meaningful analysis by type of maintained school

GCE A-Level results for History 1994

Type of School		Number of candidates	1994 Percentages achieving grades A	B	C	D	E	N	U	% A–B grades	% A–E grades	1993 % A–B grades	% A–E grades	1992 % A–B grades	% A–E grades
Comprehensive		15833	11.2	14.6	19.6	20.3	16.4	9.8	7.3	25.7	82.0	25.6	81.1	24.0	80.4
Selective		3069	18.9	20.6	21.6	18.5	10.9	5.8	3.4	39.5	90.5	37.3	89.2	35.8	91.0
Modern		157	5.1	7.0	17.8	28.0	14.6	14.6	12.1	12.1	72.6	14.8	68.9	19.5	71.9
Maintained	All pupils	19059	12.4	15.5	19.9	20.0	15.5	9.2	6.7	27.8	83.3	27.4	82.3	25.3	81.4
	Boys	8266	13.1	15.5	20.4	20.4	14.9	8.8	6.2	28.6	84.3	28.2	83.6	25.8	82.1
	Girls	10793	11.8	15.4	19.5	19.8	15.9	9.5	7.1	27.3	82.6	26.8	81.4	25.0	81.1
All subjects Maintained	All pupils		13.1	16.2	18.5	18.9	15.2	9.4	7.5	29.3	81.9	28.0	79.7	26.4	78.6

– less than 100 candidates

* more than 100 and less than 500 candidates

Printed in the United Kingdom for HMSO
Dd300299 4/95 C130 G3397 10170